IRISH MOMENTS

IRISH MOMENTS

BY BERND WEISBROD

INTRODUCTION BY PETER FITZGERALD
ESSAY BY CATHAL Ó SEARCAIGH

EDITION STEMMLE
ZURICH NEW YORK

Good photography, like a crafted story, fires the imagination of those it reaches. It never forecloses. Instead, it draws us into a reverberating, rippling interpretive process of our own. Look at Bernd Weisbrod's work. None of the photographs forces any conclusion upon you. So often, you think you have grasped an image. Then a detail may catch your eye. This part within the whole, simultaneously mundane, appropriate and jarring, sends you off again on a ceaseless search to tie down what refuses to be categorized.

Bernd Weisbrod's masterful evocation of the everyday of our lives here challenges us to re-see, re-interpret, and re-enchant. For a moment, we look out through his eyes, and we come back to ourselves better equipped to see through our own.

There's a strong sense of place evident in Bernd Weisbrod's pictures ... a strong sense of the sacredness of place. It's as if he himself made a spirited connection with his own vital creative energies in these locations; as if he found some enduring values amid the change and transience of all human things. Like the native American Indians, like Jason and the Argonauts, like the Celts themselves, who felt the urge and the need to make the ritual journey into the unknown, Bernd Weisbrod journeyed to Ireland. According to W.H. Auden, the English poet, it takes little talent to see clearly what lies under one's nose, but a good deal of it to know in which direction to point that organ. Weisbrod's instincts led him "home" to my country. Here, it seems to me, he is attuned to people and to places, both physically and psychically. But more importantly, here he is in tune with himself. For me that is what "home" is all about; to be in harmony with oneself and one's environment.

I became acutely aware of the word "home" while I was cruising around Piccadilly Circus, London, in the mid-seventies; "a hustle here, a hustle there, hey babe, take a walk on the wild side". In the amped-up lingo of Lou Reed, I was a thrill-seeking teenager, doing my best to be self-indulgently hip. But I was just a foppishly dressed yob from the back-country. I should have been a stylishly slick dude from Belgravia. Anyway, I felt uneasy being funky and as a result I began to look into that terrible dark pool of the Self, the *Duibheagán*, as I call it in Irish. At times like that you realize you're an abyss, a pitch-black pit. There's only a deep darkness. You get dizzy looking down into the gulf, the chasm of yourself. You realize there's a terrible deadening, deafening silence ... that there are no answers. A poem became for me an act of defiance thrown in the face of that silence.

I wrote in English, poems of adolescent angst, mostly. A poetry of pimples. I wrote bad poems because I didn't have the humility to read really great ones. Until one evening in the autumn of 1975, a man who worked in the storeroom of Oxford University Press walked into the pub where I worked and handed me a copy of Derek Mahon's latest collection, *The Snow Party*. That book had a profound effect on me, especially the first poem, called "Afterlives." Derek Mahon, a Belfast man, had gone to London at the beginning of the Northern Troubles and I think he felt it on his conscience that he hadn't accounted for these terrible times in his poetry. So "Afterlives" is a homecoming poem, in that Mahon came back to Belfast. The last verse was a real shock of recognition:

BUT THE HILLS ARE STILL THE SAME
GREY-BLUE ABOVE BELFAST
PERHAPS IF I'D STAYED BEHIND
AND LIVED IT BOMB BY BOMB
I MIGHT HAVE GROWN UP AT LAST
AND LEARNT WHAT IS MEANT BY HOME.

Home! The word just winged its way off the page. I felt the word as an intense desire to be reunited with something from which I felt I was cut off. The word was a smell from another world; the lost domain of my *Dúchas*. *Dúchas* is a difficult word to explain in English, but briefly it means a sense of connection; a feeling of attachment to a place, a tongue and a tradition; a belief that one belongs to a sustaining cultural and communal energy; that one has a place and a name. Suddenly I realized that I was in exile in an alien city where I neither had a face nor a name nor a place. To be an exile meant to be on my own. It meant to be without the community's sense of warmth and settledness. I had to return "home" to reclaim my heritage, my *Dúchas*. I also realized that the Irish language was my emotional language and not English. Intuitively I knew more about the texture and the tone, the aura and the soul-life of words in Irish. Irish would bring me back "home." "Home" was a discovery for me, something I removed the cover from. It had always been there ... only hidden.

For Bernd Weisbrod this journey, this quest, takes him to a place that he recognizes as home; a place where the beginning is the end and the end is the beginning. It's not only a voyage into the past and the present in order to experience a more fulfilling, vibrant future. What he's really seeking, I think, is an expanded present. These photographs are aware of the contemporaneity of all history in Ireland. They are alert to the constant presence of the past. The past is not disposed of, as we might have expected according to George Buchanan, a Northern Ireland writer; it is in a very special way still here and alive. It has entered the here and now so that it never becomes old ... however thickly the grass grows over it. We reek of the past. It can be overpowering at times to hear these megalithic rumblings from an unimaginable and sometimes unmanageable past. We have also, of course, drawn strength and sustenance from imagining and contemplating that past. Our literature is a testament to that pursuit. But what really fascinates people about Ireland is that the past is contemporary. Everyday history takes place, even when nothing happens.

Weisbrod, the Seer, sets out on his quest knowing that it is his duty to return in order to share the wonders and adventures he has experienced. The most valuable spiritual experience of the solitary being is of no social significance unless it is given back to society. These pictures are, of course, the rich rewards of Weisbrod's quest, the visual narratives of his journey. Like mythology they tell the stories of the soul; they are photographs of the Irish psyche. From Heinrich Böll's *Irish Journal*, a warm and affectionate account of my country that kindled an interest in Ireland among many Germans, Weisbrod cites, in a most charming way, some aspects of the Irish psyche that appealed to him: "When something happens to you in Germany, when you miss a train, break a leg, go bankrupt, we say: it couldn't have been worse; whatever happens is always the worst. With the Irish it is almost the opposite: (...) instead of a leg you might have broken your neck, instead of a train you might have missed Heaven, and instead of going bankrupt you might have lost your peace of mind, and going bankrupt is no reason at all for that. What happens is never the worst: on the contrary, what's worse never happens. (...) With us, it seems to me, when something happens, our sense of humor and imagination deserts us; in Ireland that is just when they come into play." These photos are visual vignettes, snapshot commentaries that clarify Böll's comments.

In Ireland we swing like pendulums between the two eternal verities of our lives: "It could be worse" and "I shouldn't worry." This photographer is an accomplished practitioner of this matter-of-fact approach. He knows that he cannot plan these photos with a fixed schedule and scheme. They happen unbidden. Like laughter, they come unlabored. It has to be a lightning-fast perception; a sighting and a click, and hope for the best. It's a "found art" dependent upon chance, the unforeseen and a certain amount of serendipity. Weisbrod may not have any Irishness in his lineage or in his lineaments but he has enough of it in his lens to be able to depict that enigmatic territory between the parish of "It could be worse" and the parish of "I shouldn't worry." There's a proverb in Irish that embodies the essence of that territory: *D'fhág mise faoi chúram Dé é is d'fhág seisean faoi mo chúram féin é*. I left it all in the hands of God and he left it in mine.

Lord Norbury was an 18th century Dublin judge. He was a hard, exacting man, by all accounts with a wicked streak of humor. Once, while condemning a man to death for stealing a pocket watch, he quipped, "You made a grab at time, idiot, but you caught eternity." A Draconian measure for such a petty crime. However, that phrase, that sentence, can be appropriated, in a more positive manner, of course, to describe the art of Bernd Weisbrod. In these photographs it seems to me that he has managed to grab the moment of recognition, the moment of revelation, in order to capture it for eternity. In a world of flux and transience he illuminates small moments with a lyrical intensity. They are experiences made vivid. For him it's a question of seeing so much clearer than the rest of us, of doing to people and places what the light does to them. Bernd has trained his eye to look with intelligence, to look intently. He is focused. He sees what other people have forgotten to see. In the Irish language the word for poet is "file." It means to see ... to be a seer. A photograph may only take a split second of execution but it represents, as Susan Sontag said, "a lifetime of preparation." A lifetime of walking around with one's eyes open. To be a good photographer you have to have eyes as sharp as tin-openers. And as with any good artist, it takes, I think, a certain amount of wisdom.

How to become wise is a quest that we are all engaged in, how to repose in the stability of truth. Once upon a time a little girl asked her grandfather how to become wise.

"I AM WISE BECAUSE I HAVE GOOD JUDGEMENT," THE GRANDFATHER SAID.

"BUT HOW DO YOU GET GOOD JUDGEMENT?"

"WELL, YOU GET GOOD JUDGEMENT FROM EXPERIENCE."

"BUT HOW, GRANDPA, DO YOU GET EXPERIENCE?"

"OH, YOU GET EXPERIENCE," REPLIED THE GRANDFATHER, "FROM POOR JUDGEMENT."

This photographer has learned his craft painstakingly. He has served a long apprenticeship of trial and error. Now he has become a master of his art; a seer who transmutes the ordinary into the extraordinary. These photos are active meditations. "They want to wake us up, not put us to sleep," as Tomas Trenstomer, the Swedish poet, remarked about poetry. They make us aware, while looking at them, of being in Life ... of being alive, in a profoundly refreshing way.

There is a reverence for Life in these photographs. They are suffused with a warmth and an affection for their subjects. There can of course be no self-respect without respect for others—no love and reverence for others without love and reverence for oneself. And isn't that what compassion is all about—an imaginative recognition and humane understanding of all life forms? It seems to me that all expressions of art need to be compassionate ... need to care. Dylan Thomas expressed it much more succinctly when he said that the joy and function of poetry is, and was, the celebration of man, which is also the celebration of God.

Above all else, this book is a journey, a cultural journey in Ireland. We are made aware that we, as a people, are local and yet international, that we are ancient and yet modern; that we are thatched-cottage-minded as well as modern-bungalow-minded. And I love such journeys—mystery tours of life and of imagination. I remember my old friend Maggie Neddie Dhonnchaidh, my next-door neighbor in Min A'Leá, a woman who never left her home except once in her lifetime, a long epic journey to West Clare on a June day in 1963—and back home again on the same day. Her sister, Biddy, was married to a Clare man and they resided in London. That year they decided to spend a holiday with his relations in County Clare, and Maggie was invited to visit them. She did, but it was a flying visit. She commanded a local driver, Charlie John Óig, to drive her there and back on the same day. From that day onwards, her favorite topic of conversation was "The day that I went to County Clare." She would recite every detail of each twist and turn of that journey, each adventure she experienced from the ordinary to the extraordinary. Every aspect of that trip was printed in her memory ... what she had seen, what she had heard and what she had felt. Years later, when my friends and I would tell her of the adventures we had had while traveling in Europe or in America, her guileless face would light up and she'd say, "Well, isn't that strange—that's exactly like what happened to me the day I went to Clare." That was her off on the journey of wonder once more. And as she got older, this one-day Odyssey became more magical and more epical. Maggie Neddie Dhonnchaidh created a myth for us in Min A'Leá, a myth that shines like a star above the daily boredom of our lives, a myth that raises our spirits when life oppresses us. We only have to think of "The day that I went to County Clare" and we know that there is an escape route from the "sad music of humanity." Alas, Maggie Neddie Dhonnchaidh is beneath the clay in Gortahork cemetery, but I'm sure that her youthful spirit is hitchhiking through eternity.

As you look at the photographs in this book, I would advise you to have your antennae aloft, the sensors of the imagination. Just like Maggie, you must be a seer on your special journey. Truth reveals itself only to those who seek it out, and you will not see it unless your eyes are open, the eyes in your head as well as those of your mind. My wish for you is that those things which were hidden will be revealed, that the dark mist will dissipate and the brilliant light illuminate your thoughts. Take a sightseeing tour of these photoscapes. You will, I hope, return to yourself, enriched.

14 THE WAY HOME · KILKIERAN · COUNTY GALWAY · 1996

16   IRISH LINEN · COUNTY DONEGAL · 1998

18 AFTERGLOW · DUNGLOE · COUNTY DONEGAL · 1998

20   Bʀɪɴɢɪɴɢ ᴛʜᴇ ᴛᴜʀꜰ ʜᴏᴍᴇ · Cᴏᴜɴᴛʏ Gᴀʟᴡᴀʏ · 1992

22   Kɪᴛᴄʜᴇɴ ᴍᴜsɪᴄ · Cᴀʀɴᴀ · Cᴏᴜɴᴛʏ Gᴀʟᴡᴀʏ · 1996

SONNY · GALWAY · COUNTY GALWAY · 1991

26   ALEC FINN · ORANMORE · COUNTY GALWAY · 1992

28   B<small>REAK</small> · G<small>ALWAY</small> · C<small>OUNTY</small> G<small>ALWAY</small> · 1996

Tony MacMahon · Rossaveal · County Galway · 1993

A FARMER'S SON · COUNTY DONEGAL · 1998

34 S<small>HEEP SHEARING</small> · C<small>OUNTY</small> G<small>ALWAY</small> · 1992

Paul Doyle · Galway · County Galway · 1993

38   NOEL SPAIN · ROS MUC · COUNTY GALWAY · 1990

A FARMER · COUNTY GALWAY · 1994

42   Cutting the turf · Casla · County Galway · 1994

44   Aʀᴀɴ Iѕʟᴀɴᴅѕ · Cᴏᴜɴᴛʏ Gᴀʟᴡᴀʏ · 1994

46 DONKEY · COUNTY SLIGO · 1993

TELEPHONE CALL · COUNTY GALWAY · 1993

50 Swan song · Galway · County Galway · 1998

Sea view III · Salthill · County Galway · 1995

54   Sᴇᴀ ᴠɪᴇᴡ I · Cᴏᴜɴᴛʏ Gᴀʟᴡᴀʏ · 1997

Salthill · County Galway · 1991

On the beach · County Galway · 1991

LIFE-GUARD · COUNTY DONEGAL · 1998

62   T<small>EMPORARY AGREEMENT</small> · S<small>ALTHILL</small> · C<small>OUNTY</small> G<small>ALWAY</small> · 1992

Pony show · Clifden · County Galway · 1992

BIG MAN · CLIFDEN · COUNTY GALWAY · 1992

Dog race · Galway · County Galway · 1996

Waterboy · Salthill · County Galway · 1994

Mullaghmore · County Sligo · 1998

HEATWAVE · GALWAY · COUNTY GALWAY · 1992

Good day for a pint · County Clare · 1992

Pᴜʙ ᴍᴜsɪᴄ · Sᴘɪᴅᴅᴀʟ · Cᴏᴜɴᴛʏ Gᴀʟᴡᴀʏ · 1993

For sale · Galway · County Galway · 1990

Noon time · Galway · County Galway · 1996

SIDE BY SIDE · DUBLIN · COUNTY DUBLIN · 1998

THE BUTCHER · COUNTY CLARE · 1990

Soap opera · County Clare · 1994

LEGION OF MARY · COUNTY CLARE · 1990

ST. PATRICK'S DAY · SPIDDAL · COUNTY GALWAY · 1993

Festival time · Milltown · County Clare · 1990

WEIGHTY · COUNTY GALWAY · 1992

THERE IS HOPE · DUBLIN · COUNTY DUBLIN · 1996

Walk · Salthill · County Galway · 1997

THE HOOKER · COUNTY CLARE · 1992

Sea view II · County Clare · 1994

Black Head · County Clare · 1992

Cliffs of Moher · County Clare · 1990

SNAPSHOT · COUNTY DONEGAL · 1998

112   MAUREEN KENNY · GALWAY · COUNTY GALWAY · 1991

EUGENE LAMBE · FANORE · COUNTY CLARE · 1993

Near the fireplace · Ros Muc · County Galway · 1996

John Behan · Moycullen · County Galway · 1993

FÁILTE · COUNTY GALWAY · 1996

Baby · County Galway · 1996

124   CHARLIE PIGGOTT · KINVARA · COUNTY CLARE · 1993

126   D̈ürer was here · County Donegal · 1998

Drive slowly · Kylemore · County Galway · 1992

Madonna · County Clare · 1993

Tomas MacEoin · Carraroe · County Galway · 1994

Muckish Mountain · County Donegal · 1998

QUIET PLACE · COUNTY GALWAY · 1991

138   TIRED · DUBLIN · COUNTY DUBLIN · 1998

140   Yvonne Flynn · Turloughmore · County Galway · 1993

THE BURREN · COUNTY CLARE · 1992

144   Double vista · County Galway · 1991

146 WEDDING DAY · SPIDDAL · COUNTY GALWAY · 1992

Nice place · Carraroe · County Galway · 1991

THE FENCE · COUNTY DONEGAL · 1998

152   Min A'Leá · County Donegal · 1998

154 JOHNNY CONNOLLY · INVERAN · COUNTY GALWAY · 1993

156

Bernd Weisbrod

first traveled to Ireland—with backpack and tent—in 1976. Captivated by the island's landscape and its people, he was equally fascinated by the gradual changes taking place in highly traditional Irish society. He has since journeyed frequently to Ireland to capture images both typical and unique with his camera. The exhibition *Irish Moments* has been presented at several different locations, including Galway, Ireland. Born in Ludwigshafen on the Rhine in 1952, Bernd Weisbrod now lives in Ingelheim, near Mainz. He studied photography at the Folkwangschule in Essen. Afterwards he worked as theater photographer and taught photography at the University of Mainz. A freelance photographer, he works primarily in the realms of theater, cabaret, fringe shows and the visual arts and often takes on major photographic themes.

CATHAL Ó SEARCAIGH

was born in the Irish-speaking part of County Donegal, where he lives on a farm today. He was educated at the National Institute for Higher Education in Limerick and in Maynooth, has spent time in London and Dublin and traveled extensively. He was Writer-in-Residence in Coleraine, Belfast and Galway. Publications include: *Miontragéide Chathrach*, poems, 1975; *Truilingt*, poems, 1979; *Suile Shuibhne*, poems, 1983; *Suibhne*, poems, 1988; *Mairimid leis na Mistéiri*, stage play, 1989; *Tá an Tóin ag titim as an Lsaol*, stage play, 1994; *An Bealach 'na bhaile*, poems, 1991; *Homecoming, Selected Poems*, 1993; *Oiche Gealai I nGaililé*, stage play, 1995; *Na Buachailli Bána*, poems, 1996; *Out in the Open*, poems, 1997. He is a member of "Aosdána," a group of artists supported by the Irish State, and has received various awards.

PETER FITZGERALD

is author and editor of *CIRCA*, a magazine devoted to literature and the arts. He lives and works in Dublin.

Reproduction copyright by Bernd Weisbrod, Ingelheim (Mainz), Germany
Text copyright by the authors
Editorial direction by Mirjam Ghisleni-Stemmle, Andreas Ritter, Marko T. Hinz
Layout by Alexandra Weller, Baar-Zug, Switzerland
Printed by Kündig Druck AG, Baar-Zug, Switzerland
Bound by Buchbinderei Burkhardt AG, Mönchaltorf-Zurich, Switzerland

ISBN 3-908161-69-X